HOW TO FIND INFORMATION

•

SOCIAL SCIENCES

By JENNIE GRIMSHAW

THE BRITISH LIBRARY

How to find information: social sciences

ISBN 0-7123-0868-7

Published by:
The British Library
96 Euston Road
London NW1 2DB

British Library Cataloguing-in-Publication Data
A catalogue record is available for this book from the British Library

Desktop publishing by Concerto, Leighton Buzzard, Bedfordshire
Tel: 01525 378757

Printed in Great Britain by Atheneum Press Ltd, Gateshead, Tyne and Wear

Contents

Introduction

This booklet aims to provide practical guidance to social science researchers and practitioners on how to locate the information they need.

The guide is divided into thirteen main chapters, each covering a different kind of information source. It describes, briefly, how each category of tool can be used to trace a different sort of information, ranging from the contact details of a research institute to research findings on a social problem or issue. By consulting the appropriate chapters researchers can learn how to select and use the best information sources to find the data they need. All the information sources featured in the guide have been chosen on the basis of being particularly useful, or representative samples of what is available.

Researchers should find that the searching approach recommended in this guide is useful in any public or academic library with a good social science collection. The guide is aimed at researchers using library collections and concentrates on the sources they are most likely to find available in library reading rooms, with a particular emphasis on electronic forms of publication.

Chapter 1. Libraries

Before starting your research, you may need to identify an appropriate library or libraries operating in your field, and to which you can gain access. There are a number of directory publications that will enable you to do this. The four in regular use in the British Library's Social Policy Information Service and kept reasonably up to date are:

- *The Aslib Directory of Information Sources in the United Kingdom*, 10th ed. London: Aslib, 1998. This most comprehensive directory of libraries is updated about every two years. The tenth edition contains over 11,500 entries, giving details of address, opening hours, subject coverage, access arrangements, and publications produced for each institution. Libraries are listed in alphabetical order, but there is an extensive subject index.

- *Libraries in the United Kingdom and the Republic of Ireland*, London: Library Association. Annual. This smaller directory covers public and academic libraries in the UK comprehensively and government and special libraries selectively. It gives full contact details for each institution, but no note of their subject coverage. A subject index is, however, provided.

- *Guide to Libraries and Information Units in Government Departments and Other Organisations*, 33rd ed. London: British Library, 1998. This guide does not aim to be exhaustive in coverage, but emphasises libraries within government departments and similar agencies (including overseas government agencies and official bodies located in the UK). It also includes other selected organisations whose collections are relevant to subjects which may be of interest to government bodies and others with similar information needs, and which are prepared to accept serious enquiries from outside. For the most part these are public bodies, regulatory bodies, charities, trade associations and selected institutions recognised as being a national authority in a particular field. Entries give contact and access details and quite extensive descriptions of stock and services. Libraries are listed alphabetically, with indexes by subject and organisation. The publication is regularly updated, and a new edition is due out next year (2001).

- *Parliamentary Holdings in Libraries in Britain and Ireland* by D.L. Jones and C. Pond, Westminster: House of Commoms Library, 1993. Social science researchers needing access to Parliamentary material will find the union list of holdings compiled by the House of Commons Library invaluable in locating collections in their area. It was compiled as a statement of British and Irish holdings at a time when a number of collections were being weeded or disposed of, and is based on returns received during the Autumn/Winter of 1992/93. A new edition is currently in preparation.

Of course, the UK's largest collection of social science material is held by the British Library. Its Social Policy Information Service (SPIS) acts as the focus for the exploitation of these collections by personal users of the London reading rooms and remote enquirers. Social science researchers wishing to use the Library's reference services may contact us by letter, phone, fax or email:

Social Policy Information Service
British Library
96 Euston Road
London NW1 2DB
Tel.: 020 7412 7536
Fax: 020 7412 7761
Email: social-policy@bl.uk

Chapter 2.   How to Find What Published Sources Exist

At the beginning of your research you will need to identify key organisations active in the field, available abstracting and indexing databases, the main current awareness services, major journals and relevant books. The following chapters will mention a range of sources that you may find helpful. They represent only a small part of what is actually available. To identify a more comprehensive range of information sources in a particular subject, indexes and directories should be used. Some of the most comprehensive of these are listed below.

Identifying books

Commercially published books are the easiest information source to identify. Relevant titles can be easily found by searching the catalogue of your own library and the catalogues of other academic and research libraries which are available on the Internet. Catalogues of libraries in this country and beyond which are mounted on the Web can be accessed via BUBL UK, a directory of organisations and institutions, at **http://www.bubl.ac.uk**. The British Library's catalogues are available free at our website at **http://www.bl.uk**.

Identifying journals

Scholarly journals, trade magazines and newsletters remain primary means of accessing academic research results and keeping up with new developments in the field. There are two major directories widely available that may help you to identify publications which you might like to scan regularly.

- *Ulrich's International Periodicals Directory*, New Providence, NJ: Bowker. Annual. Ulrich's has established itself as the premier serials reference source in the world. It contains information on nearly 161,200 serials published throughout the world, classified and cross-referenced under 974 subject headings with indexes by title and International Standard Serial Number (ISSN). It includes trade and academic journals and newsletters currently available, as well as directories, statistical series and annual reports and reviews. The growth of electronic publishing is reflected, with 14,757 online electronic journals and 4,958 serials available on CD-ROM being covered in the 2000 edition. The directory itself is available in numerous electronic formats, including Ulrichsweb.com on the Internet, Ulrich's on Disc from R.R. Bowker, and Ulrich's International Periodicals Directory CD-ROM from SilverPlatter Information.

- *Willings Press Guide*, Teddington: Hollis Directories. Annual. This smaller directory covers UK titles in vol.1 and the rest of the world in vol.2. The primary arrangement is alphabetical by title for the UK, with indexes by subject. Willings has been available on CD-ROM from 1999.

Identifying electronic media

The growth of information in electronic form has been exponential, but for an overview of what is out there, why not try:

- *New Media Titles*, London: Waterlow New Media Information. Annual. The Waterlow New Media Information guide aims to be a single source of comprehensive and accurate information on electronic media products. The current edition lists more than 32,000 currently available CD-ROM, DVD and other new media titles and their publishers, split into academic, professional and consumer titles. Titles are arranged alphabetically within each section, with an index by broad subject. The database is also available free at the company's website (**http://www.newmediainfo.com**) and on the New Media Information CD-ROM.

- *Gale Directory of Databases*, Detroit, Mich: Gale Group. Twice a year. This product profiles more than 14,000 databases available worldwide in a variety of formats. Vol.1 of the print version describes online databases while vol.2 covers CD-ROM, diskette, magnetic tape, batch access and hand-held products. Descriptions are very full and include information on subject coverage, content, time span, updating frequency and contact details. Titles are arranged alphabetically, with an index by subject. The directory is also available as a CD-ROM from SilverPlatter.

- *Searching CD-ROM and Online Information Sources* by G.G. Chowdhury and S. Chowdhury. London: Library Association Publishing, September 2000. This forthcoming text claims to alert users to the breadth of information available in CD-ROM and online format. It evaluates a range of electronic sources and explains corresponding search and retrieval techniques in a way that should prove invaluable to anyone battling with the bewildering range of electronic information sources available.

Identifying directories

To trace the existence of a directory of organisations active in your field, two main sources are available:

- *Current British Directories*, 13th ed., Beckenham: CBD Research, 2000. Irregular. This lists directories published in the British Isles alphabetically, with indexes by subject and publisher. 'Current' is flexibly interpreted to allow the inclusion of directories which, though to some extent dated, are still useful or are to be published in new editions in the near future. Entries are fairly full and give information on publisher, frequency, contents and formats available.

- *Directories in Print*, Detroit, Mich.: Gale Group. Annual. The current edition describes 15,422 active rosters, guides, and other print and non-print address lists published in the United States and worldwide. It consists of descriptive listings arranged under 26 broad subject categories, with subject, title and keyword indexes. Descriptions are detailed and include information on coverage, arrangement, indexes, updating frequency and publishers' contact details.

Chapter 3.   Directories

One way of 'finding out' in the social sciences is to approach organisations or people active in the field and ask for help, advice and information. There are a wide range of general and specialist directories available to help in this in both print and electronic form. A good directory should enable you to find out:

- Contact details for organisations and/or individuals working in your field

- The scope of an organisation's activities

- Whether or not the organisation has a library or information service

- Whether or not the organisation produces a newsletter

The following illustrative examples will give a flavour of what is available to help you track down organisations operating in the social sciences generally:

- *Directory of Social Research Organisations in the United Kingdom*, 2nd ed., edited by M. Bulmer, W. Sykes and J. Moorhouse. London: Mansell, 1998. This valuable reference guide covers individual independent researchers, academic institutions, professional associations and learned societies, philanthropic foundations, and training courses. For each organisation it provides contact details, and a description of its history and activities.

- *Directory of British Associations*, 14th ed. Beckenham: CBD Research, 1998. This standard reference work is also available on CD-ROM. It provides information on national associations, societies and institutes that have a voluntary membership in all fields of activity. It is arranged alphabetically, with indexes by subject. For each organisation it gives contact details, services provided, and a note of serial publications produced.

- *Councils, Committees and Boards*, 11th ed. Beckenham: CBD Research, 1999. This is a handbook of advisory, consultative, executive, regulatory and similar bodies in British public life, arranged alphabetically with a subject index. For each body it gives contact details, history, remit and publications produced.

- *Centres, Bureaux and Research Institutes*, 4th ed. Beckenham: CBD Research, 1999. Includes details of 2,000 establishments in Britain serving a wide variety of interests including the social sciences arranged alphabetically with a subject index, an index of abbreviations and an index of 90 university sponsors.

- *Voluntary Agencies Directory*, London: National Council for Voluntary Organisations. Annual. Gives information on the national voluntary sector in England, with agencies listed alphabetically and indexed by subject. Each entry provides a note of the organisation's objectives, services and contact details.

- *Charities Digest*, London: Waterlow Professional Publishing. Annual. Gives a brief note, in alphabetical order of organisation, of the charity's objectives and contact details, with an index by subjects.

- *Guide to Pressure Groups*, 2nd ed. London: PMS Publications, 1997. Covers pressure groups, think-tanks, public affairs consultancies and political organisations in the UK. Gives contact details, history, objectives, staff and publications produced for each organisation.

- *CommunityWise*, CD-ROM, Caterham: Oxmill Publishing. Quarterly. The community organisations file includes details of a wide range of community groups and organisations in the UK, indexed by subject, activities and location.

- *World of Learning*, London: Europa Publications. Annual. Gives listings by country of research institutes, libraries, learned societies and universities worldwide. All entries provide contact details, principal personnel, activities and publications information. Also available on CD-ROM.

- *Civil Service Year Book*, London: The Stationery Office. Annual. One way of tracing government activity in policy development is to identify and bother the civil servant(s) responsible. The main tool for identifying these is the *Civil Service Year Book* which gives names of senior personnel and a contact telephone number for divisions, directorates and units within ministries and government agencies for England, Scotland, Wales and Northern Ireland. The Year Book is available in both print and CD-ROM formats.

- *Yearbook of International Organisations*, Munich: Saur. Annual. Detailed organisation descriptions appear in alphabetical order with indexes by subject and a country directory of secretariats and memberships. For each organisation the directory gives contact details, history, structure, activities and publications produced. Also issued on CD-ROM.

Beyond these general directories there are a plethora of works covering specific social science fields. A few illustrative examples are given below:

Local Government

- *Municipal Year Book*, London: Newman Books. Annual.

Social Services

- *Social Services Year Book*, London: Financial Times Pitman Publishing. Annual.

- *Guide to the Social Services*, London: Waterlow Professional Publishing. Annual.

Health care

- *IHSM Health and Social Services Year Book*, London: Financial Times Business Directories. Annual.

- *Binley's Directory of NHS Management*, Corringham, Essex: Beechwood House. Three issues yearly.

Education

- *Education Year Book*, London: Financial Times. Annual.

- *Directory of Vocational and Further Education*, London: Financial Times. Annual.

- *Continuing Education Year Book*, Leicester: National Institute of Adult Continuing Education. Annual.

- *Commonwealth Universities Year Book*, London: Association of Commonwealth Universities. Annual.

Children

- *ChildData CD-ROM*, London: National Children's Bureau. Quarterly. The organisations' directory file gives detailed information on ca. 3,700 national and international organisations concerned with children.

Older people

- *Age Info CD-ROM*, London: Centre for Policy on Ageing. Quarterly. Includes an organisations' database containing references to over 3,000 organisations active in the field of older people in the UK, Europe and worldwide.

Penology and criminology

- *Police and Constabulary Almanac*, Henley-on-Thames: Hazell. Annual.

- *NAPO Probation Directory*, Crayford, Kent: Shaw. Annual.

- *Shaw's Directory of Courts in the United Kingdom*, Crayford, Kent: Shaw. Annual.

Chapter 4.   Encyclopaedias

When starting research in a new area it can be useful to orient yourself by consulting an encyclopaedia or handbook to get an overview of your subject and a digest of current knowledge. A wide range of encyclopaedias is available on various aspects of the social sciences, and some obvious criteria need to be used to assess their reliability and authority:

- How old is the book? (many encyclopaedias are updated very infrequently and may contain out of date and misleading information)

- Are the articles written by people with proven expertise in the field?

- Do the articles include bibliographies?

- Does the work show national bias, eg is it written from an American point of view?

- Is there a good index?

- Is the work aimed at the specialist or the lay person?

No general encyclopaedia of the social sciences has been published since the *International Encyclopaedia of the Social Sciences* edited by David Sills appeared in 1968. However, help is at hand in the shape of an ambitious project by Pergamon to develop an *International Encyclopaedia of the Social and Behavioural Sciences* that will describe the state of knowledge in all the disciplines in the field. This mamoth work is scheduled for publication in September 2001 in print and electronic form. It will comprise 4,000 commissioned articles and will include around 90,000 bibliographic references as well as comprehensive name and subject indexes. Those wishing to follow its progress towards completion can visit its website at **http://www.iesbs.domino.com**

The following specialist encyclopaedias are cited simply as illustrative examples of what is available based on those in regular use in the Official Publications and Social Sciences Reading Area at the British Library. The list is not intended to be exhaustive.

Economics

- *International Encyclopedia of Economics* edited by F.N. Magill. London: Fitzroy Dearborn, 1997. This work aims to provide the non-specialist reader with insight into topics often accessible only to academics and experts in a very abstruse field. The 393 articles included cover economic theory, economic systems, economic history, econometrics and statistics, economic development, monetary and fiscal policy, international economic relations, and industrial, welfare and labour economics.

Education

- *Encyclopedia of Special Education: a Reference for the Education of the Handicapped and Other Exceptional Children and Adults*, 2nd ed., edited by C.R. Reynolds and E. Fletcher-Janzen. New York: Wiley, 2000. Written from an American point of view, this handy reference contains biographies, descriptions of educational and psychological tests, reviews of interventions and service delivery, and information on handicapping conditions.

- *International Encyclopedia of Education*, 2nd ed., T. Husen and T. N. Postlethwaite (editors-in-chief). Oxford: Pergamon, 1994. This massive 12 volume work attempts to present an overview of international research and scholarship in the fields of educational problems, theories, practices and institutions. While the articles on theoretical topics like 'attention in learning' give a good introduction to the subject, descriptions of national education systems are obviously only valid up to 1994. Further information in this case must be sought elsewhere!

Political organisations

- *Encyclopedia of British and Irish Political Organizations: Parties, Groups and Movements of the Twentieth Century* by P. Barberis, J. McHugh and M. Tydesley. London: Pinter, 2000. This invaluable work provides succinct information on a very wide range of political organisations and movements which had significance in Britain and Ireland in the last century. Each entry gives a brief history of the movement and its ideals, together with a note of any serial publications it issued. We have found even the most obscure bodies listed!

- *Encyclopedia of World Terrorism*. Armonk, N.Y.: Sharpe, 1997. Describes terrorist groups and campaigns by region and country. Also covering state responses to terrorism, and giving an historical overview of terrorist campaigns ancient and modern, the encyclopaedia provides a good general introduction to the subject, with a select bibliography.

Psychology

- *Encyclopedia of Psychology* edited by A.E. Kazdin. American Psychological Association/OUP, 2000. A combination of historical, descriptive, synthetic, and analytic articles cover topics ranging from educational, clinical and experimental psychology to developmental, personality, organisational/industrial and social psychology as well as psychoanalysis and cross-cultural psychology. This work summarises international research in over 1,500 entries written by 1,200 scholars from 50 countries.

Social conditions

- *Encyclopedia of Social Issues* edited by J.K. Roth. New York: Marshall Cavendish, 1997. Provides basic information about, and discussion of, a broad range of controversial subjects in the fields of politics, economics, human rights, the environment, medicine, law and religion. Again, this work is written from an American point of view.

Social policy

- *International Encyclopedia of Public Policy and Administration*, J.M. Shafritz (editor-in-chief). Boulder, Colo: Westview Press, 1998. This work represents a major effort toward the international integration of the literature on public policy and administration. It includes articles on all of the core concepts, terms, phrases and processes of budgeting, comparative public administration, industrial/organisational psychology, industrial policy, international trade, labour relations, public management, organisation theory and behaviour, policy analysis, political economy, political science, public administration and finance, and taxation. It offers a combination of historical descriptive articles, procedural presentations and interpretive essays.

Social work

- *Encyclopedia of Social Work*, 19th ed., R.L. Edwards (editor-in-chief). Washington, DC: National Association of Social Workers, 1995 + 1997 Supplement. Brings together, again from an American point of view, scholarly analyses of a broad range of social problems and social work practice interventions.

Sociology

- *International Encyclopedia of Sociology*, edited by F.N. Magill. London: Fitzroy Dearborn, 1995. This work is aimed at the lay person and presents information in an easy-to-understand style. The 338 articles in the encyclopedia follow a standard format for ease of use. They begin with ready-reference information stating the kind of sociology and particular field of study to which the subject belongs. Next a brief summary describes the topic's significance and defines key terms. This is followed by the main text of the article in three sections: Overview, Applications and Context. An annotated bibliography follows this section, followed by cross-references to related material elsewhere.

Chapter 5.   Grey Literature

Grey literature is defined within the British Library's Document Supply Centre as 'literature which is not readily available through normal bookselling channels, and therefore difficult to identify and obtain'. Examples of grey literature include research reports, working papers, conference proceedings and preprints, dissertations, trade literature and so on. Uncertain availability is only one characteristic of grey literature: others include non-professional layout and format, low print runs and non-appearance in mainstream published bibliographies and indexes. We will consider here three categories of grey literature of particular importance to social scientists.

Research and practice reports

These consist of accounts of research and development work issued by university departments, think-tanks, pressure groups, independent and government sponsored research institutes, and voluntary sector organisations. They are informally published in short print runs or on ephemeral websites by the research organisation itself and are not available through commercial booksellers. Because they are difficult and time-consuming to trace, they are not widely collected by libraries. When held in the collection of a large research library, they will almost certainly not be individually catalogued but will appear under the name of the issuing body plus a generic title such as 'working papers' or 'Occasional publications' eg:

*   University of Liverpool, Centre for Central and Eastern European Studies. Working papers. Rural transition series. 1-.

Research and practice reports are, however, targeted more by the smaller special libraries serving professional and voluntary sector bodies and independent research institutes operating in a closely defined field. These are inclined to acquire and catalogue relevant reports individually rather than as part of a series and to index them intensively. Specialist indexing and abstracting tools produced by such libraries based on their own collections are therefore good sources for tracking grey materials. The organisations will also generally allow access to their libraries to bona fide researchers needing to consult hard-to-find documents, although a fee may sometimes be charged.

Access to report literature does have many advantages for the enquirer as it provides up to date information on the progress of research. Being informally published, and not subject to peer-review, reports offer researchers a much quicker way of disseminating results than through academic journals. A researcher may have to wait for up to two years for an article to be published in an academic journal, whereas a research report can be mounted on a website in days or printed in a few weeks. In many cases the information in the report literature will be far more detailed than that which appears in journal articles. Finally, it is a mistake to think that information issued in informal documents will eventually reappear in a journal article. A large proportion of results reported in grey publications are never formally published.

All British report literature acquired by the British Library is added to the National Reports Collection which is managed by the Library's Document Supply Centre as a corporate and national resource. It can be traced through:

- *British National Bibliography for Report Literature*, 1998 –, Wetherby, West Yorks: BSDS Publications. Monthly. Formerly *British Reports, Translations and Theses*, 1981-97. Unfortunately this is time-consuming to search in hard-copy since it is arranged by very broad subject categories with rudimentary keyterm indexing and does not cumulate. Basically, one has to scan sequentially.

- *SIGLE* CD-ROM, 1980 –, London: SilverPlatter. Quarterly. The System for Information on Grey Literature in Europe (SIGLE) CD-ROM includes all material covered by the *British National Bibliography for Report Literature* plus the output of the other European Union countries. Records do not carry verbal subject headings, so searching is largely by free text keywords. They do, however, include uncontrolled terms giving additional keyword access if it is felt that the title is insufficiently descriptive. Up to three very broad subject category codes are also assigned to each record, a list of which can be found in the printed BNBRL described above. These can be used in conjunction with keywords to refine searches. In spite of its serious limitations for subject searching, SIGLE is the most comprehensive bibliography of grey literature that we have and and has the additional benefit of indicating from where the documents can be obtained.

For US grey literature in the realm of public and social policy, it is worth trying:

- *PolicyFile*, Alexandria, Va: Chadwyck-Healey. Weekly. PolicyFile is a unique subscription-based database produced by Chadwyck-Healey US, indexing research and practice reports covering the complete range of public policy. It draws its content from public policy think-tanks, university research programmes and research organisations. Some well-known contributors include the Brookings Institution, Carnegie Endowment for International Peace, Cato Institute, Economic Strategy Institute, Hoover Institution, Hudson Institute, International Monetary Fund, National Center for Policy Analysis, OECD, Rand Corporation and the World Bank. The database can only be accessed online via the Internet, and therefore is able to provide hotlinks to full text of documents when these are available on the Web. It also offers links to the home pages of sponsoring organisations and to their email addresses from within individual document records. Although the service is at present heavily biased towards American research, Chadwyck-Healey UK are actively considering developing a British version, so watch this space! For further information visit the PolicyFile website at **http://www.policyfile. com**.

Grey literature in the field of education, mainly but not exclusively that originating in the US, is announced in:

- *Resources in Education*, 1975-, Washington, DC: USGPO. Monthly. Formerly *Research in Education*. *Resources in Education* (RIE) is sponsored by the Educational Resources Information Center (ERIC) of the Office of Educational Research and Improvement of the US Department of Education. It consists of comprehensive document descriptions with extensive abstracts and indexes by subject, personal author, institution and publication type. Subject coverage is wide and includes fringe subjects such as psychology, sociology, information science, statistics and computing. The bibliographical database which embraces ERIC activities consists of two files, *Resources in Education* and *Current Index to Journals in Education* (CIJE) which treats published journal literature from over 700 periodicals. The combined database goes back to 1966 and is available in CD-ROM form from several providers, including SilverPlatter and Knight Ridder. In the UK, ERIC documents can be obtained from the British Library Document Supply Centre.

There are also a range of databases produced by specialist libraries in the UK and based on their own collections which will include the research and practice reports they have acquired. These are described in detail in the chapter on Abstracting and Indexing Sources, but include:

- *ChildData*, CD-ROM and Online

- *AgeInfo*, CD-ROM

- *CareData*, CD-ROM and Online

- *Urbadisc*, CD-ROM and Online

- *CommunityWise*, CD-ROM

Conference papers

Researchers may also choose to announce their results in papers delivered to meetings, the proceedings of which may or may not be published. Conference proceedings may be published commercially as books, appear in academic journals or be issued informally. The best source for verifying whether or not the proceedings of a meeting have been published is:

- *Index of Conference Proceedings*, 1964-, Wetherby, West Yorks: British Library Document Supply Centre. Monthly with annual cumulations.

This contains records of over 350,000 conference proceedings held at the BLDSC going back to the year 1787.

This source will simply confirm the fact that a meeting took place, but to find out what went on at a conference it is necessary to identify the subject content of individual papers. This can be accomplished by looking at either or both of the following two resources.

- *InsideWeb Database*, Wetherby, West Yorks.: British Library Document Supply Centre. This online resource is again produced by the British Library Document Supply Centre and is available as a fee-based service via the Internet. It provides paper level details from the conference proceedings received by the BLDSC from 1993 and is updated daily. Material cited in the the InsideWeb database and in the conference index is available on interlibrary loan from the British Library Document Supply Centre through your local public or college library.

- *Index to Social Sciences and Humanities Proceedings*, Philadelphia, Pa.: Institute for Scientific Information. Quarterly, with annual cumulations. The *Index to Social Science and Humanities Proceedings* (ISHP) is a unique resource which provides access to both proceedings and the papers which appear in them. ISHP indexes the most significant published proceedings from throughout the world from a range of disciplines in the social sciences and humanities. Important proceedings in foreign languages are included as well as those in English. The Contents of Proceedings section gives a complete bibliographic description of each set of proceedings and lists the papers presented and their first author. There are indexes by broad category, by subject terms taken from titles of papers and books, by sponsor, by author/editor, and by meeting location. The product is available on CD-ROM and online as well as in print format.

Theses

In the UK, universities have adopted a very conservative approach to the provision of copies of theses, although the BLDSC has a collection of doctoral dissertations going back to 1970. Additions are announced in the *British National Bibliography of Report Literature* and its predecessor *British Reports, Translations and Theses* and are included in the SIGLE database.

To verify details of British or Irish theses, whether held in the BLDSC or not, consult:

*   *Index to Theses with Abstracts accepted for Higher Degrees by the Universities of Great Britain and Ireland*, 1950-, London: Aslib. Quarterly. Now available on the Internet at **http://www.theses.com**. From the Index, it is possible to ascertain what theses have been submitted and then apply direct to the universities in question for permission to examine them.

The best source for identifying theses from North America is:

*   *Dissertation Abstracts International. Section A. Humanities and Social Sciences*, 1861-, Ann Arbor, Mich.: Bell and Howell Information and Learning. Monthly. DAI includes bibliographical details and an author-prepared abstract of up to 350 words in length, which describes in detail the research project upon which the dissertation is based. Most of the dissertations included in DAI can be purchased on microfilm or as paper copies. DAI is also available on a monthly CD-ROM from SilverPlatter and on a quarterly CD-ROM or online from Bell and Howell themselves. The Bell and Howell website at **http://www.umi.com** offers free access to the last two years of the DAI database and an online ordering facility called Dissertations Express.

Chapter 6.   Current Awareness Services

It is not practicable for researchers to keep up to date by personally scanning all journals and books published in their fields for items of interest. It can take six months to a year for citations of journal articles to appear in the major abstracting databases. Enterprising publishers have therefore produced a range of current awareness services to alert researchers quickly to new developments in their field. There are two major current awareness services which cover the social sciences, and certain publishers are offering innovatory alerting services by electronic means.

- *InsideWeb*. Inside offers a fully integrated current awareness and document ordering service via the Internet which allows you to search, order and receive documents held by the British Library Document Supply Centre. It covers 20,000 of the world's most valued research journals (of which c.7,000 relate to the social sciences) and includes a Table of Contents service from which the contents details of any journal included on the database can be sent to subscribers by email on a daily, weekly or monthly basis. The information is extremely current as Inside is updated on a daily basis. Bibliographic details of articles with author abstracts where available are added to InsideWeb less than 72 hours from receipt of any new journal issue.

- *Current Contents. Social and Behavioral Sciences.* This resource, produced by the Institute for Scientific Information (ISI), displays tables of contents from more than 1,580 journals and books and provides complete bibliographic data for every item covered: articles, editorials, letters, commentaries and reviews. It is available on the Web, on CD-ROM or in print, updated weekly. Selling points include:

  - English language author abstracts (in electronic formats)

  - Searchable author keywords (in electronic formats)

  - Author and publisher addresses

  - Document delivery service

  - Customised alerting service that allows the subscriber to create personalised profiles and receive regular, targeted alerts (Web version).

- *Web of Science*. If you do not have access to Current Contents, ISI's *Web of Science Database* (WOS) can easily be used as a current awareness tool. The *Web of Science Database* is available online via the Internet and indexes academic journals in the pure and applied sciences, the social sciences and the humanities. The introductory screen of the WOS full search option will allow you to limit your search to records added this week, in the last two weeks or the last four weeks. You can combine this limit with a subject search to find the most recent articles on your research topic.

Alerting services

A number of publishers of scholarly journals are beginning to offer free alerting services for the contents of the journals they produce. SARA (Scholarly Articles Research Alerting) delivers by email the contents pages of any of the academic journals published by Carfax, Spon, Psychology Press or Taylor and Francis in advance of publication. Over 500 peer-reviewed journals in a variety of disciplines are covered. For those journals which are available online, the email will contain links to the online contents. You can register your interest in this complimentary service via the Taylor and Francis website at **http://www.tandf. co.uk/journals**. ContentsDirect is a similar service from Elsevier which delivers book and journal tables of contents directly to your PC in advance of publication. Imprints covered by this service are Elsevier, Pergamon, North Holland and Excerpta Medica. Subjects include social sciences, economics and management science. You can choose as many book subject areas and journal titles as you like and register online at **http://www.elsevier.nl/locate/ contentsdirect**.

Specialist sources

As well as the general current awareness services we have just looked at, a wide range of specialist services are available from a number of niche providers, often voluntary organisations or research institutes operating in a particular field. The sources listed here are mostly in hard copy and, with the exception of the Greater London Authority Research Library bulletins, reasonably priced in the £30.00–£50.00 per year range. The GLA Library bulletins are more expensive, being aimed at organisations rather than individuals.

- **Greater London Authority Research Library**. The GLA Research Library collects books, reports, journals, statistical series and newspapers in the fields of urban and regional planning, housing, social policy, local government finance and policy, education and training, leisure and recreation, and economic development. Based on these collections, the Library produces a range of alerting services designed to bring relevant information to your attention monthly, fortnightly, weekly or even daily. The *Daily Information Bulletin* offers concise abstracts of articles in quality daily newspapers and press notices. A series of subject specific briefing bulletins gives in-depth coverage of new developments and emerging topics. Titles available include *Education Bulletin* (fortnightly), *Labour Market Bulletin* (monthly), *Social Services Bulletin* (fortnightly), *Housing Abstracts* (fortnightly), *Planning and Transport News* (fortnightly) and *Local Management and Finance* (fortnightly). *Urban Abstracts* (monthly) provides an authoritative summary of the most recent reports, books and journal articles acquired by the Library arranged under broad subject headings for easy scanning.

- **National Institute for Social Work Information Service**. *Caredata Abstracts* from the NISW Information Service provides a monthly guide to recent literature on social care and social work. It lists and abstracts books, central and local government reports, research papers, publications of voluntary organisations, and journal articles, and also summarises the latest news items and practice developments in the social care field. It is arranged under broad subject headings to facilitate browsing. It is also available free on the Internet from January 1999 at **http://www.nisw.org.uk**, thanks to funding from the Department of Health and the Scottish Executive.

- **Department of Health Library and Information Services**. *Health Service Abstracts* is a monthly bulletin that gives bibliographic details and summaries of books, book chapters, reports, journal articles and other publications on the non-clinical aspects of health services, with major emphasis on the UK. It includes sections listing NHS reports from Health Authorities and Department of Health publications, and usually incorporates a list of recent NHS Executive circulars.

- **National Children's Bureau**. The NCB produces a range of alerting services, including *Highlights*, *ChildData Abstracts* and *Children in the News*. The *Highlights* are an occasional series of bulletins summarising recent research findings, influential reports and important legislation. *ChildData Abstracts* is a monthly list of new books, reports, pamphlets and journal articles added to the NCB Library's catalogue. *Children in the News* is a weekly abstracting service that looks at the main issues affecting children and young people as reported in the national press. It is available by post, fax or email.

- **Centre for Policy on Ageing**. *New Literature on Old Age* is published six times a year as a guide to all new publications on ageing and old age. It covers not only new books and periodical articles, but also central and local government reports and circulars, statistical reports, semi-published research documents, and informal publications issued by voluntary groups. Giving comprehensive coverage of literature from the UK, it also includes publications from other European countries, the USA and the rest of the world. Forthcoming courses, conferences and seminars are annnounced.

- **Royal National Institute for the Blind**. *New Literature on Visual Impairment* is published every two months. It takes in all aspects of visual impairment, including health care, education, social provision, rehabilitation, daily living, recreation and leisure, and literature on special groups such as deafblind and multiple disabled people. The listings include books and journal articles, government reports and papers, grey literature and many ephemeral items. Bibliographical details, but not abstracts, are given.

- **British Institute of Learning Disabilities**. The *BILD Current Awareness Service* is a monthly bibliography designed to keep people up to date with everything that is new in the field of learning disabilities. It lists new books and resources, journal articles and audio-visual materials, together with details of forthcoming educational events, current projects, new schemes, and organisations.

- **Planning Exchange**. The *ISLA Bulletin* is a selective document produced weekly which contains about 35-40% of the materials collected by the Planning Exchange in the preceeding 10-14 days. It covers local government, education, housing, planning, social services, transport and infrastructure, economic development and urban and rural regeneration. Full bibliographic descriptions and detailed abstracts are given for all items recorded. The *Housing Information Digest* provides a current awareness service on all aspects of housing and is published monthly. As well as providing abstracts of the books and research reports acquired by the Planning Exchange Information Unit, it also includes abstracts of articles from around 500 journals, each issue of which is scanned regularly, a section on Parliamentary Questions relating to housing issues, a news page and events and seminars notices. Entries are arranged by broad subject for convenience of scanning. A back-up document supply service is available for subscribers. Content is drawn from the Planning Exchange's Planex database. Access to this online resource is available on a subscription basis but is very expensive. It is unlikely to be available in your local library!

Current journals

One of the best ways of keeping up to date with current developments is regularly to scan the leading 'trade' journal in your field. Its news section will announce the publication of interesting research reports, government policy initiatives, etc. Here are a few of the relevant titles listed by subject:

Economics	*Economist*. Weekly
Education	*Times Educational Supplement*. Weekly
	Times Higher Education Supplement. Weekly

Employment	*Working Brief* (Unemployment Unit and Youth Aid). Monthly
	Labour Market Trends (National Statistics). Monthly
Health care	*Health Service Journal.* Weekly
Housing	*Roof* (Shelter). Bi-monthly
	Housing (Chartered Institute of Housing). Monthly
Local government	*Local Government Chronicle.* Weekly
	Municipal Journal. Weekly
	Public Finance. Weekly
Parliament	*House Magazine.* Weekly
Race relations	*Runnymede Bulletin* (Runnymede Trust).
Social care	*Community Care.* Weekly

Chapter 7.   Current Research

If you want to find out about people active in research in the social sciences, and about research currently in progress, the standard resource is:

*   *Current Research in Britain. Social Sciences.* Baltimore, Md.: Community of Science, Inc. Annual.

Indexes research in progress at institutions and their departments by name of researcher and by subject. The 1999 edition is the last that will appear in parallel print and CD-ROM versions. The publication will henceforth be available in electronic form only.

Information about the research programmes they sponsor can also be found at the websites and in the bulletins and directories issued by major funding bodies such as the Economic and Social Research Council (ESRC). Basic information about ESRC funded programmes can be found at their website at **http://www.esrc. ac.uk**. Outputs from ESRC funded research can be found in their REGARD database at **http://www.regard.ac.uk**. Using REGARD, you can search for details of ESRC research awards and the publications and research activities which are the products of these awards. Finally, the bulletin *Social Sciences – News from the ESRC,* published three times a year in hard copy, provides up-to-date information about ESRC policies, new research and findings from completed research.

The websites of most university departments will usually include information about their current research programmes. Links to social science departments of academic institutions both in the UK and abroad can be found in the Grapevine section of the Social Science Information Gateway (SOSIG) at **http://www. sosig.ac.uk**.

Research updates in both print and electronic form covering specific sectors are also available. The Institute for Volunteering Research's *Research Bulletins*, which summarise results of recently completed projects, are available at its website, **http://www.volunteering.org.uk**. The *CommunityWise CD-ROM* produced quarterly by Oxmill Publishing includes a database of current and recent social action research projects based on information supplied by the Joseph Rowntree Foundation and the National Centre for Volunteering.

The Joseph Rowntree Foundation is a major funder in the area of social research. Its website at **http://www.jrf.org.uk** provides access to a database of projects in progress which you can search by keyword, researcher surname, organisation, project title and programme. Full text of summaries of the results of completed projects are also available from the Findings database at the website.

Community Care magazine produces a twice-yearly paper digest entitled *Research Matters* summarising recent research results in the fields of residential care, older people, social security, carers, family life, child protection, mental health, learning difficulties and disability, youth justice and poverty.

Promising new initiatives to raise awareness of research in progress in particular fields include a call by the National Institute for Social Work for people voluntarily to register their current research in a publicly available database at their website at **http://www.nisw.org.uk**. The Family Policy Studies Centre and the National Family and Parenting Institute are working together to prepare a national map of family and parenting research currently being carried out in the UK. They intend to produce a paper directory of ongoing research as well as an electronic version. Watch this space! In the area of local government, the Local Government Association (LGA) has recently taken over from the Improvement and Development Agency responsibility for the support of research. It will be producing regular electronic bulletins on research activity and outputs in the field. For information on the development of the new service, check the LGA website at **http://www.lga.gov.uk**.

At the international level, CORDIS is the European Community Research and Development Information Service. It provides access to information on research, development and innovation taking place on a European level in all subject fields. Its website at **http://www.cordis.lu** contains news on European Union-funded research programmes and initiatives. Also available are a number of searchable databases. These include news, research programmes, projects, and results, acronyms used in research and development and lists of partners for possible European collaboration.

The World Bank disseminates information about the research projects it sponsors in the development area via its website at **http://www.worldbank.org**. The site offers an alphabetical list of projects by title, searchable databases of abstracts of current studies, evaluations of research and Policy Research Working Papers in full text. A number of the research projects offer a free email newsletter, to which you can subscribe via an online form at the website. Finally, the *World Bank Policy and Research Bulletin* published quarterly informs the development community of the Bank's policy and research output. The bulletin is available at the Bank's website, with an archive of past issues from 1990.

The secret as ever is to identify organisations active in your specialist field, and to contact them directly or to check out their websites, where their activities will be proudly made known.

Chapter 8.   Statistical Information

Access to statistical data is vital for researchers needing to track social and demographic trends. The complex and often overlapping social, economic and business mechanisms of the 1990s mean that decision-making in government, commercial, and non-profitmaking organisations is becoming more important but also more difficult. One element in good decision-making and in achieving an understanding of social processes and problems is access to accurate and up to date statistical data.

The published statistics most useful to social scientists are those produced on a regular basis that allow changes over a period of time to be measured. Such statistics are produced by a variety of bodies and are generally divided into 'official' and 'non-official' statistics. 'Official statistics' are collected and published by central government departments, or by a national statistical office acting on behalf of those departments or by inter-governmental organisations. 'Non-official' sources encompass all those statistics produced by organisations outside central government, including trade and professional associations, academic institutions, banks, private research companies and local authorities.

However, most statistics are out of date as soon as they are published because it takes time to collect, process and issue the data. Few statistical publications tell users what is happening now or what is likely to happen in the future.

The methodology used to collect data for statistical series usually varies from one series to the next and, in turn, these differences will affect the final results. The methodology may also change over time in a specific time series making it difficult to compare figures in one series from one period with those in another period.

Official statistical data in particular are often published in summary form. More detailed figures are held by statisticians in the collecting department and may be made available on request. It is always worth asking, although payment of a fee for the additional information may be required.

Data require effective analysis and interpretation if the information is to be useful. Any statistical series can be interpreted in a number of ways, while specific elements of the series can be excluded or given more weight in the final analysis. A statistical series, however well produced, can be misunderstood. While there is no doubt that data can be deliberately manipulated and misinterpreted, in other cases the different interpretations are genuine and result from the nature of time series data and the legitimate emphasis given to particular items in the series.

Statistics today can be published in hard copy format, appear on the websites of the collecting organisations, or be available in machine-readable form as manipulable datasets. Published 'official' and 'non-official' statistics are voluminous. This guide will prudently confine itself to pointing out some useful guides and directories of what exists!

UK sources

The first port of call for anyone wishing to track down British official statistics is:

- *Guide to Official Statistics*. 2000 edition. London: TSO, 2000. This provides a comprehensive directory of all the statistical censuses, surveys, administrative systems, press releases, publications, databases, CD-ROMs and other services managed by the statisticians working in the Government Statistical Service and the Northern Ireland Statistics and Research Agency. It is produced on an occasional basis, so does tend to get out of date, but the new edition published this year is invaluable in providing an overview of what exists and current contact details for the statisticians responsible for collecting and publishing the datasets, who generally do not mind being telephoned.

National Statistics, launched in June 2000 as the successor to the Office for National Statistics, offers the free online Statbase service, which provides access to a comprehensive set of key official statistics. It gives detailed descriptions of all the UK Government Statistical Service's data sources, derived analyses, statistical products and services, and relevant contact points. It also offers the TimeZone service which allows access to individual time series from the range of statistical data produced by government and its agencies. Its Textsearch facility allows you to make a keyword search for both datasets and printed products.

The National Statistics DataBank is a subscription-based service for complete macroeconomic datasets. The 55,000 datasets available are drawn from a variety of government departments and the Bank of England.

To access both the StatBase and DataBank services, visit the National Statistics website at **http://www.statistics.gov.uk**. The site has been redesigned following the launch of the independent National Statistics agency. It is now organised around 13 separate themes, each dealing with a distinct area of national life and corresponding to the chapters in the *Guide to Official Statistics*. It also includes a selection of the latest economic indicators and *UK In Figures*, a sample cross section of data showing how we live in the UK today.

In addition, all the major UK central government departments have a statistical arm, many of which have their own Web presence. The result is a wealth of statistical data freely available on the Internet in various formats. The best guide to the websites of the main UK statistical bodies is found in:

- *Official UK: the Essential Guide to Government Websites* by D. Jellinek, London: Stationery Office, 1998. For the latest revisions of the book, see its accompanying web page at **http://www.official-uk.co.uk**

Members of the academic community needing access to manipulable statistical datasets should contact the Data Archive (formerly known as the ESRC Data Archive) at the University of Essex which houses the largest collection of machine-readable datasets in the social sciences in the UK. It is a national resource centre, disseminating data throughout the UK and internationally. Founded in 1967, it currently houses approximately 5,000 datasets of interest to researchers. For further information about the service, and to access its catalogue, BIRON, visit its website at **http://www.data-archive.ac.uk**

Researchers needing access to questionnaires used in a number of major British social surveys should visit the Question Bank website at **http://qb.soc.surrey. ac.uk**. The resource is produced by the Centre for Applied Social Surveys and offers questionnaires used by the Census of Population, British Social Attitudes Survey, General Household Survey and Labour Force Survey, among others.

Finally, researchers wishing to consult UK statistics at the level of region, constituency or local authority should turn for guidance to:

- *SubNatStats 1999: a Subject Index to Sub-national Statistics*, J. Fitches and I. Grove (editors). London: London Research Centre, 1999. The index covers statistical series that are currently published on a regular or occasional basis, and that relate to urban planning, social policy and local government issues. Census publications are excluded.

International statistics sources

There is a growing demand for access to international and comparative statistics as the world shrinks to a global village. Statistical publications of inter-governmental organisations (IGOs) are essential sources of basic information on the population, business and financial activities, foreign trade, education, health and other economic, demographic and political characteristics of nations and world regions. These publications contain data reported by the statistical bodies of national governments throughout the world, or collected by IGOs themselves through field research or co-operative data exchange programmes. They often include cross-national comparisons to the extent that such comparisons can be made, and virtually all are published in English as well as other languages. They can be traced through the following three reference sources.

- *Index to International Statistics, 1983-*, Bethesda, MD: Congressional

Information Service. Monthly, cumulated quarterly and annually. The IIS:

- identifies the statistical publications of major inter-governmental organisations as they are issued

- provides full bibliographic information for each

- describes the statistical contents of each publication, including the context and level of detail in which data are presented, data sources and time coverage

- indexes this information in full subject and geographical detail.

The resource is also available in online form as part of the CIS Statistical Universe database. For further information visit the website at **http://www. lexis-nexis.com/cispubs**.

- *Global Data Locator* by G. T. Kurian, Lanham, MD: Bernan Press, 1997. This is a user's guide and road map to global statistical information sources, which provides annotated and descriptive reviews and tables of contents for 240 statistical publications produced by both official and commercial organisations. It covers both print and electronic publications.

- *INSTAT: International Statistics Sources*, London: Routledge. Irregular. INSTAT covers more than 400 statistical sources published by both private and public bodies. It is organised by subject rather than by source. Subjects are analysed at two levels: a cross-classification of 46 broad subject areas in the overview, and detailed topical breakdowns of these 46 subject areas. All publications are referred to by code in the body of the book. Full bibliographic details arranged by these codes are given in Appendix A.

Researchers seeking international compilations of historical statistics may use:

- *International Historical Statistics. Europe, 1750-1993*. 4th ed. by B. R. Mitchell, Basingstoke: Macmillan, 1998.

- *International Historical Statistics. The Americas. 1750-1993*. 4th ed. by B. R. Mitchell, Basingstoke: Macmillan, 1998.

- *International Historical Statistics. Africa, Asia and Oceania, 1750-1993*. 3rd ed. by B. R. Mitchell, Basingstoke: Macmillan, 1998.

These invaluable compilations of nationally produced data cover population, labour force, agriculture, industry, external trade, transport and communications, finance, prices, education and national accounts.

The main source for European Union statistical material is Eurostat, the Statistical Office of the European Communities. A list of their statistical publications can be found at the website of EUR-OP, the Office for Publications of the EU, at **http://eur-op.eu.int**. Eurostat's own website at **http://europa.eu.int/en/ comm/eurostat/serven/home.htm** gives free access to press releases, key economic indicators, publications catalogues and database information. The site has been recently redesigned and can now be searched by keyword or browsed by theme. The jewel in the Eurostat crown for the social scientist is New Cronos, an online database of social and economic statistics, covering not only member states but also Japan, the US and central European countries. Researchers who are prepared to pay can request searches for specific information via the Eurostat Data Shops network, or by faxing back a form downloaded from the website. Results can be delivered on diskette, printout or CD-ROM.

Members of the academic community needing to look beyond the Essex Data Archive for access to manipulable datasets may approach the Inter-University Consortium for Political and Social Research (ICPSR) which provides access to the world's largest archive of computer-based research and instructional data for the social sciences. The data holdings cover a broad range of disciplines including political science, sociology, demography, economics, history, education, gerontology, criminal justice, foreign policy and law. ICPSR member institutions pay annual dues that entitle staff and students to acquire the full range of services offered. Individuals at non-member schools can also order data for an access fee. For further information visit the ICPSR website at **http://www.icpsr.umich. edu**.

Finally, inter-governmental organisations put up varying amounts of statistical data free on their websites. For hotlinks browse SOSIG, the Social Science Information Gateway, Statistical Section on the web at **http://www.sosig.ac.uk**.

Statistics of foreign countries

The first port of call for tracing statistical information about an individual foreign country is their statistical yearbook, which will include abstracts of the main data series covering all aspects of national life. These will be found listed in:

- *Guide to official publications of foreign countries*, 2nd. ed, G. Westfall (editor), Government Documents Round Table, American Library Association, 1997.

For those needing to identify more detailed information sources, the following may help:

- *Statistics Europe*, 6th ed. by J. M. Harvey, Beckenham: CBD Research, 1997. This work is arranged in alphabetical order of country. Each country section contains contact details for the central statistical office and principal libraries, bibliographic descriptions of principle statistical series by subject group and a note of the main bibliographies of statistical publications.

- *Statistics Sources*, Detroit: Gale Group. Annual. This publication is a subject guide to data on industrial, business, social, educational, financial and other topics for the US and other countries worldwide. US statistical series are indexed by subject; those relating to other countries under the name of the state.

- *World Directory of Non-Official Statistical Sources*. 2nd ed., London: Euromonitor, 1998. This directory covers statistical sources in the areas of consumer goods markets, key industrial sectors, and national economic and business trends produced by a range of organisations including trade associations, financial institutions and market research companies worldwide. It provides details of 2,800 regularly published titles across 90 consumer and industrial sectors, including a description of coverage, frequency of publication, and publisher contact information.

US statistical series can be traced using two complementary indexes:

- *American Statistics Index, 1972-*, Bethesda, MD: Congressional Information Service. Monthly, cumulating annually. The ASI identifies statistical data published by all branches and agencies of the US Federal government, provides full bibliographic descriptions and indexes the material by subject.

- *Statistical Reference Index, 1980-*, Bethesda, MD: Congressional Information Service. Monthly, cumulating annually. The SRI covers statistical publications issued by major US associations and institutes, business organisations, commercial publishers, independent research centres, state government agencies and universities. Information is indexed by subject, issuing body and title.

Both of these indexes are also available online as part of the CIS Statistical Universe database. For further information visit the CIS website at **http:// www.lexis-nexis.com/cispubs**.

Finally, most national statistical agencies will have a presence on the Web, from which one can find information about their publications and services, plus some free data. Eurodata, the website of the Mannheim Centre for European Social Research, at **http://www.mzes.uni-mannheim.de/eurodata** carries links to European and selected North American government statistical agencies. The Governments on the website at **http://www.gksoft.com/govt/en** also provides links to national statistical offices worldwide.

Chapter 9.   Official Documents

Government policy and its impact on society is an area of prime concern for social science researchers and practitioners. To trace the evolution of a policy in any country, the researcher will need to penetrate the labyrinth of its official material. This guide will confine itself to describing in outline how to retrieve UK government material, with only the briefest mention of the vast subject of how to trace and access the output of foreign national governments and the European Union.

UK sources

UK government documents will enable you to trace the evolution of an idea from its appearance in a green paper at the consultation stage, through its formulation as a policy statement in a white paper to its enshrinement in law through the legislative process.

UK government documents can be divided into Parliamentary and non-Parliamentary material. Parliamentary material itself falls into two categories: sessional papers which consist of the information papers required by Parliament in its work of legislation and of monitoring government, and the proceedings, of which the two most important series are the Journals of each House and the Debates of each House.

Parliamentary papers

The House of Commons sessional papers will be most used by social scientists and currently fall into three series:

- **Public bills** – draft Acts of Parliament.

- **House of Commons papers** – papers generated within the House, notably reports of Select Committees, papers required by Acts of Parliament to be submitted to Parliament, eg annual reports of some public bodies, and papers submitted to the Commons in response to requests from it for information.

- **Command papers** – policy documents submitted to Parliament by the wish of the government. Also known as white papers.

The proceedings of Parliament are of two types – a record of what has been done, reported in the Journals of either House, and a record of what has been said, reported in the Debates of both Houses, commonly called *Hansard*.

Non-Parliamentary material consists of legislative documents and the range of consultation papers, research and practice reports, guidance material and statistics, etc. put out by individual government departments and agencies. The privatisation of HMSO in 1996 accelerated an already existing tendency for government departments to publish this material themselves informally rather than through the official government publisher, so that it is becoming increasingly difficult to track down and acquire. This material is also increasingly distributed in electronic form on government websites, where it remains only as long as it is current and topical, without benefit of archiving.

Guides and indexes

Parliamentary publications are well covered by the commercially produced guides and indexes and most libraries holding sets will not have attempted to catalogue individual papers. Non-Parliamentary publications will in many cases have been catalogued individually or as series by libraries acquiring them. For both categories, identification will be facilitated by use of the guides and indexes recommended here:

- *The Stationery Office (TSO) (formerly HMSO) daily list and monthly and annual catalogues.* These have been produced since 1836 and are still available in hard copy from TSO. The TSO catalogue and daily list can also be accessed through its website at **http://www.ukstate.com**. However the online catalogue at the website is not archival and is designed to support sales of current publications only. It is not a substitute for the permanent record of HMSO/TSO documents found in the printed lists.

- *United Kingdom Official Publications Index* (UKOP). This is a bibliographic database covering TSO publications, material published directly by official organisations and publications of international organisations distributed by TSO from 1980 to the present. It is available from Chadwyck-Healey as a bi-monthly CD-ROM or online. The online version of the product will be developed into a full text archive of UK national government material covering all documents in the following categories: press releases, factsheets and guidance documents, circular letters, consultation papers, statistics, annual reports, inspection reports, and inquiry reports. The archive will include both documents freely available on the Web and digital versions of documents issued in print form. Visit their website at **http://www.chadwyck.co.uk** for more information.

- *British Official Publications Current Awareness Service* (BOPCAS). This web-based service currently contains over 16,850 references drawn from the extensive Ford Collection of British Official Publications at the University of

Southampton. The database covers Acts of Parliament, Parliamentary papers and departmental publications from 1995 and includes full bibliographic details and subject keywords. Subscribers also have the benefit of subject-based email alerting services and links to full text of documents where these are available on the Internet. For more information, visit the BOPCAS website at **http://www.bopcas.com**.

- The *Weekly Information Bulletin* (WIB) is the most useful guide to the current business of the House of Commons and is also in part an index to its publications. It contains details of the business of the House for the previous week and forthcoming business of both Houses for the fortnight following; details of legislation as it proceeds through Parliament; details of Standing and Select Committees and their publications; and lists of White Papers, Green Papers and EU documents received. At the end of the session some of this information is cumulated in the *Sessional Information Digest* (SID). Both the SID and the WIB are available from the Stationery Office in print form and can also be found on the Internet via links from the UK Parliament home page at **http://www.parliament.uk**.

- *Justis-Parliament* is a bibliography and index to the proceedings of both Houses of Parliament from 1979 to the present day. As well as indexing the Official Report (*Hansard*) and the Parliamentary Papers, it also includes the text of Early Day Motions, Parliamentary Questions and their answers and bill histories. The database is drawn from the POLIS database prepared by the House of Commons Library for its own internal use and is published by Context Electronic Publishers. The current database (1992 to date) is available both on CD-ROM and online. Archives for the periods 1979-1987 and 1987-1992 are available on CD-ROM only.

Current government documents are increasingly available in full text on the Internet. The *Guidelines for UK Government Websites* published in December 1999 require that all public sector organisations should publish command papers, consultation documents, research reports, statistical information, and regulatory and guidance material on their websites. However, government regards the Internet as a medium for the presentation of current information, and policies for archiving are not well developed. This means that documents published electronically may not be available in perpetuity.

The principal gateway for Internet access to UK governmental information is the Central Computer and Telecommunications Agency (CCTA) Government Information Service (GIS) website at **http://www.open.gov.uk**. This provides an alphabetical listing of government departments and agencies, a topic index by broad subject and access to the Infoseek search engine. For a printed guide to, and review of, government websites, use:

- *Official UK: the essential guide to government websites* by D. Jellinek. London: TSO, 1998. The latest revisions of this book will be found at its accompanying web page at **http://www.official-uk.co.uk**.

European Union sources

As European integration gathers pace, EU law and policy are having an ever greater impact on the UK. European Union documentation is extremely complex and researchers would be best advised to contact their nearest specialist information provider for help with the identification of material.

There are three depository libraries in the UK where a comprehensive collection of EU official documentation is held. These are:

Westminster Central Reference Library
35 St Martins Street
London
WC2 7HP
Tel: 020 7461 4634

Business and Information Library
William Brown Street
Liverpool
L3 8EW
Tel: 0151 233 5829

British Library
Document Supply Centre
Boston Spa
Wetherby
West Yorkshire
LS23 7BQ
Tel: 01937 546060 (Customer Services)

Material held by the British Library Document Supply Centre is available through the national network for interlibrary lending via your college or local public library. A reference enquiry service is not offered.

European Documentation Centres (EDCs) receive a complete range of EU documentation and are based in universities to serve the academic sector. European Information Centres (EICs) provide information on European Union issues to business and ensure that companies' queries are answered quickly and effectively. Some services are subject to a charge.

Up to date contact details for EDCs, EICs and other sources of European Union information are found in:

- *European Public Affairs Directory*, Brussels: Landmarks. Annual.

The principal gateway for European Union information on the Internet is the Europa server at **http://www.europa.eu.int**. This site gives access to the home pages of the major EU institutions, including the European Commission, the European Parliament, the European Court, the Economic and Social Committee, etc. As the website is complex and can be bewildering to the novice, guidance on how to make best use of it and other online sources is found in:

> *The Directory of Online European Information*, 4th ed. Brussels: Landmarks, 2000. This guide includes extensive information on almost 900 sources. It covers online databases, CD-ROMs and diskettes, as well as providing a comprehensive guide to finding your way around European information on the Internet.

Foreign national governments

A detailed explanation of how to identify and retrieve information from the output of other national governments is beyond the remit of this booklet. However, those needing to venture can find systematic descriptions of what exists for each country in:

- *Guide to Official Publications of Foreign Countries*. 2nd ed., G. Westfall (editor), American Library Association Government Documents Round Table, 1997. The Guide covers the main document series produced by each national government in the fields of legislation and legislative proceedings, court reports, statistical yearbooks, economic affairs (including the budget), census documents, health, labour market, education and environmental policy. However, its definition of 'foreign countries' naturally excludes the US and includes the UK!

For tracing government websites worldwide, consult the Governments on the website maintained by Gunnar Anzinger at **http://www.gksoft.com/ govt/en**. This database contains links to governmental institutions that provide information on the Internet, including parliaments, law courts, government agencies (ministries, offices, councils, committees, research institutes, etc.), embassies, consulates and political parties.

Chapter 10. Free Internet Sources

The quantity of information offered free on the World Wide Web has exploded over recent years to the point of becoming bewildering. The Internet has been compared to a huge library with no shelving and no cataloguing or indexing system at whose door a large lorry-load of books is dumped every hour. One of the main difficulties for the researcher is finding pearls in the shape of sites offering good quality information among vast quantities of rubbish. The second major difficulty is the transience of information published on the Web. As documents become non-current, websites are redesigned and institutions are restructured, material is constantly being removed from the Web and lost forever (the average life of a website is estimated to be 44 days, *Scientific American* Mar. 1997). There are printed guides to Internet information sources which offer reviews of sites, but things change so quickly that these are out of date almost before they are published. They are therefore excluded from this guide, which will concentrate instead on web-based resource directories and information gateways.

Social Science Information Gateway (SOSIG)

The leading resource guide for the social sciences is the SOSIG Internet Catalogue located at **http://www.sosig.ac.uk**. This is an online catalogue of high quality Internet resources. It offers users the chance to read descriptions of resources available over the Internet and to access those resources directly. The catalogue points to thousands of resources, each of which has been evaluated and described by a librarian or academic. Disciplines covered include economics, education, government, law, management, politics, psychology, social welfare, sociology, statistics and women's studies. The catalogue can be searched by keyword or browsed. Browsing allows you to see all the resources under a particular subject heading.

SOSIG also offers a number of subject guides which give information about Internet resources available in different social science subjects. These are available in html, Word 6.0 and RTF formats and can be downloaded for free from the Subject Guide Index.

Grapevine, the people-oriented side of SOSIG, offers the social science community a place to look for and publicise information about events, career development opportunities and professional colleagues. You can use Grapevine to post your CV for others to browse, seek research profiles of like-minded professional colleagues, find out about available courses and forthcoming conferences, and contact university social science departments.

NISS Directory of Networked Resources

Aimed at the academic sector, the NISS Information Directory of Networked Resources at **http://www.niss.ac.uk** takes the form of a subject-based resource guide covering all disciplines. Users are led down the branches of a hierarchical inverted subject 'tree' to the exact subject in which they are interested. Users may also browse topics in alphabetical order or Universal Decimal Classification (UDC) shelfmark order, or search by keyword or UDC classmark. Once they have found a potentially relevant resource, users are able to examine a summary description before connecting to it. NISS aims to be inclusive of all UK information sources, but coverage of the rest of the world is selective.

Infomine

Infomine at **http://infomine.ucr.edu** is offered by the University of California as a resource for the introduction and use of Internet sources of relevance to students and academics. It covers the humanities, social sciences, business, education, news, general reference and library services. The librarian-built file contains over 900 resources including electronic text archives and journals as well as online subject guides, databases and reference resources.

BUBL LINK

Bubl Link at **http://bubl.ac.uk** is a catalogue of selected Internet resources covering all academic subject areas and classified according to the Dewey Decimal Classification (DDC). All items are selected, evaluated, catalogued and described. Links are checked and fixed each month. The catalogue can be browsed by alphabetical subject headings, by Dewey Decimal Classification codes, by country or by resource type or searched by keyword.

The BUBL LINK catalogue currently holds over 11,000 resources. This is far smaller than the databases held by major search engines, but it can provide a more effective route to information for social science subjects as the rubbish is screened out.

Pinakes

The Pinakes site maintained by Heriot-Watt University at **http://www.hw.ac. uk/libWWW/irn/pinakes/pinakes.html** provides links to major subject gateways compiled by the UK Electronic Libraries Project and other bodies. These include Psych Web (Psychology), CAIN (Conflict studies), NetEc (Economics) and RUDI (Urban design) as well as SOSIG in the social science area. Associated with the Pinakes site, and also produced by Heriot-Watt University, is a free monthly Internet Resources Newsletter at **http://www.hw. ac.uk/libWWW/irn**. This provides listings of new websites used by academic researchers and reviews of print publications about the Internet.

Free Pint

Free Pint is a free email newsletter giving you tips, tricks and articles on how and where to find reliable websites and search more effectively. It is written by information professionals in the UK and is sent to more than 27,000 subscribers around the world every two weeks. The website at **http://www.freepint.co. uk** gives access to an archive of over 100 articles going back to 1997, reviews of web-related books and news about the online industry and the Internet.

The Scout Report

The Scout Report is the flagship publication of the Internet Scout Project based at the University of Wisconsin-Madison. It is produced by a team of librarians and subject specialists who select, evaluate and describe Internet resources and is published every Friday on the Web and by email. It offers a fast, convenient way of staying informed about valuable resources on the Internet in the fields of business and economics, science and engineering and the social sciences. As well as the current alerting service, there is a searchable archive of over 9,000 website descriptions. These can be searched by keyword or browsed by alphabetical subject heading. Visit the Scout website at **http://scout.cs.wisc.edu** for free access.

Free databases

Some providers are generous enough to make their subject-based abstracting and indexing databases available free on the Web. The main drawbacks of these are that the search interfaces are sometimes unsophisticated, with much less functionality than the fee-based versions, and that free access may be a temporary phenomenon. However, they are well worth knowing about and currently include:

* **Alcoholism**
  ETOH. Coverage: late 1960s-; 100,000 + records. Website: **http://etoh. niaaa.nih.gov**. The Alcohol and Alcohol Science Database (ETOH) is the most comprehensive online resource covering all aspects of alcohol abuse and acoholism. Produced by the National Institute on Alcohol Abuse and Alcoholism, ETOH contains approximately 100,000 records. It offeres indexed abstracts of journal articles, books, dissertations, conference papers, research reports and chapters in edited works from the late 1960s to the present, as well as historical research literature.

* **Education**
  AskERIC. Coverage: almost 1 million records; 1966-. Website: **http:// ericir.syr.edu/Eric**. See Chapter 11 for a detailed description of the ERIC database.

NCBE Database. Coverage: 20,000 + documents. Website: **http://www. ncbe.gwu.edu/bibliographic.** This database produced by the National Clearinghouse for Bilingual Education provides access to bibliographic citations and abstracts of materials from a variety of sources dealing with all aspects of the education of linguistically and culturally diverse students in US schools. Topics covered include curriculum and instruction, parent and community relations, teacher training and professional development, educational research, cultural diversity, and systemic reform.

- **Health economics and management**
  HealthSTAR. Coverage: 1975-. Website: **http://igm.nlm.nih.gov.** Covers the health care administration and planning aspects of health care delivery from a US perspective. *HealthSTAR* contains relevant bibliographic records from Medline (1975 to the present) together with records emphasising health care administration selected and indexed by the American Hospital Association, records emphasising health planning from the National Health Planning Information Center (1975-1991) and records emphasising health services research selected and indexed by the National Information Center on Health Services Research and Health Care Technology. The database includes journal articles, research reports, conference papers, books and book abstracts.

  NHS Economic Evaluation Database. Coverage: 1994-. Website: **http:// nhscrd.york.ac.uk.** Database of structured abstracts of economic evaluations of health care interventions produced by the NHS Centre for Reviews and Dissemination, University of York.

- **Population**
  Population Index. Coverage: 1986-1999. Website: **http://popindex. princeton.edu:80/index.html.** *Population Index*, published since 1935, is the primary reference tool for the world's population studies literature, covering books, journals and working papers. The paper version of *Population Index* has been discontinued with effect from the last issue of 1999. The Office of Population Research is exploring alternatives for continuing the electronic version of the Index. In the meantime, the archival file will remain available at the above website.

Evaluating resources

As well as using portals, gateways and alerting services, everyone surfs the Web using commercial search engines such as AltaVista, Lycos or InfoSeek. This way, vast quantities of raw information can be retrieved very quickly, but some of it will be of questionable quality and reliability. It is well worth investing a little time in developing skills in evaluating Internet resources so that you do not run the risk of degrading your work by using poor quality information or citing mis-information. The Virtual Training Suite tutorials available at **http://www.vts. rdn.ac.uk** provide an introduction to the issues of information quality on the Internet and teach the skills required to evaluate the quality of an Internet resource. The tutorials are subject specific and will also enable you to discover how to improve your Internet search skills, and to reflect on how to use the Internet effectively to support your study or research. Currently available tutorials cover economics, politics, psychology, sociology, and social work.

Online discussion groups

As well as providing free access to a wealth of information, good, bad and indifferent, the Internet can be used to facilitate communication between researchers through online discussion groups. Mailbase is the service which runs electronic discussion lists for UK academics and support staff. A group of people who share a common interest such as occupational stress or welfare reform will join a list and use email to talk to one another. You can join a list by contacting Mailbase. Your details are added to your chosen list, and you then get all messages sent to the list by other members. You can send your reply to all list members or just to one person on the list. All open (publically available) lists appear on the Mailbase website at **http://www.mailbase.ac.uk**. You can search for a relevant list by keyword, or browse by subject.

Chapter 11. Abstracting and Indexing Services

Publication in peer-reviewed academic journals is the traditional way of disseminating research results. The peer-review system is designed to assure the quality of the material published and the journals themselves are widely available in print and electronic form in research libraries or on loan from the British Library Document Supply Centre. However, academic journal articles as sources of information do have their drawbacks:

- delays of up to two years between an article's acceptance for publication and its actual appearance in the journal;

- bias towards publication of positive results with negative outcomes being suppressed;

- pressure on academic researchers to publish more in order to secure funding, leading to a deterioration in the quality of articles and the recycling of information;

- bias towards the publication of articles by leading figures in the field.

In spite of these drawbacks academic journals remain a prime source of social science information. Accessing the content is made easy by the existence of the range of sophisticated, commercially published abstracting and indexing services that are reviewed here. Most of these are available in print and electronic form, but I concentrate here on the electronic versions which offer immense advantages over print in speed and sophistication of searching. In all of the databases reviewed here, with the exception of Social Sciences Citation Index, the bibliographic records include subject indexing terms. Relevant subject search terms can be selected from browsable indexes or thesauri to increase the precision of searching and minimise the retrieval of irrelevant material. Searches can be limited to specific fields such as author or title, to works in specific languages and to those published within specific date ranges.

General databases

- **CommunityWise CD-ROM**
  Source and available from: Oxmill Publishing
  Frequency: Quarterly
  Print equivalent: None
  Contains seven reference databases including: *Community Abstracts* which comprises indexed abstracts on a wide range of social policy and welfare issues from data provided by the Community Development Foundation, the

National Centre for Volunteering and the National Youth Agency; *International Development Abstracts* which comprises references to books, journal articles and reports on all aspects of economic and social development supplied by the British Library of Development Studies and the Overseas Development Institute; *Community Organisations* which gives details of a wide range of community groups and organisations in the UK; and *Research in Volunteering* which contains descriptions of over 1,100 recent social action research projects in the UK and Europe.

* **Wilson Social Sciences Abstracts**
Source: The H.W. Wilson Company
Available from: SilverPlatter and H.W. Wilson
Frequency: Monthly
Coverage: Abstracts from 1994; Indexing from 1983
Print equivalent: *Social Sciences Index*
Offers cover-to-cover indexing and abstracting of more than 415 English language periodicals in the areas of anthropology, criminology, economics, law, geography, policy studies, psychology, sociology, social work and all urban studies. It is available as an index only, as indexed abstracts, and as indexed abstracts plus access to the full text of about 150 journals.

* **Sociological Abstracts**
Source: Cambridge Scientific Abstracts
Available from: SilverPlatter
Frequency: Quarterly
Coverage: 1963 to the present
Print equivalent: *Sociological Abstracts*
Provides access to the latest findings worldwide in theoretical and applied sociology and social policy. It features abstracts of articles from scholarly sociological journals worldwide, abstracts of conference papers presented at Sociological Association meetings, and dissertation listings.

* **International Bibliography of the Social Sciences** (IBSS)
Source: British Library of Political and Economic Science of the London School of Economics
Available from: SilverPlatter
Frequency: Quarterly
Coverage: 1951 to the present
Print equivalent: *International Bibliography of the Social Sciences*
Based on the collections of the British Library of Political and Economic Science, IBSS indexes the information contained in 2,600 social science journals and 6,000 books each year. Coverage is based on the core disciplines of anthropology, economics, political science and sociology and reflects the

increasingly interdisciplinary nature of the social sciences. Subjects covered include anthropology, business, crime, culture, demographics, economics, education, foreign affairs, government, history, law, political science, public administration, psychology, religion and sociology.

- **PsycLIT**
  Source: American Psychological Association
  Available from: SilverPlatter
  Frequency: Quarterly
  Coverage: 1887 to the present
  Print equivalent: *Psychological Abstracts*
  The American Psychological Association's PsycLIT database consists of more than 1.4 million records from 1887 to the present, covering the academic, research and practice literature in psychology from more than 45 countries in over 30 languages. It offers citations with abstracts to scholarly journals in psychology and the behavioural sciences. As well as all aspects of psychology, the database covers the behavioural aspects of education, law, medicine, sociology, social work, criminology and management.

- **PAIS International**
  Source: Public Affairs Information Service
  Available from: SilverPlatter
  Frequency: Quarterly
  Coverage: 1972 to the present
  Print equivalent: *PAIS International in Print*
  This database covers issues of current debate in the fields of economics, finance, law, international relations, public administration, government and politics, with an emphasis on matters that are or may become the subject of legislation. It contains abstracts of journal articles, books, conference proceedings, research reports and government documents worldwide.

- **Applied Social Sciences Index and Abstracts (ASSIA)**
  CD-ROM and Online
  Source and available from: Bowker-Saur
  Frequency: Quarterly
  Coverage: 1987 to the present
  Print equivalent: *Applied Social Sciences Index and Abstracts*
  Offers bibliographic references with abstracts from over 600 English language journals in the applied social sciences, including 25 of the 30 most cited sources.

- **Social Sciences Citation Index** (SSCI)
  This resource is produced by the Institute for Scientific Information and is available in hard copy, on CD-ROM and on the Internet (as part of the Web

of Science). It indexes more than 1,725 peer-reviewed journals spanning fifty disciplines, as well as covering individually selected, relevant items from over 3,300 scientific and technical journals. The database offers a novel and unique approach to subject searching, called the cited reference search. This enables you to trace articles which have cited a known book or article in their bibliographies. The thinking is that works included in an article's bibliography are most likely on the same subject as the article itself. For example, any article which includes Clegg and Wall's A Londitudinal Field Study of Group Work Redesign, *Journal of Occupational Behaviour*, vol.2, 1981 in its bibliography is likely also to be about stress management. Through a cited reference search, therefore, you can discover how a known idea or theory has been confirmed, applied, improved, extended or corrected.

Databases covering particular subjects

Supplementing these general sources there are a wide range of abstracting and indexing databases covering particular disciplines. Some of these are commercially produced while others are based on the collections of a range of specialist libraries. The comprehensiveness of the latter in covering their field is liable to be variable and to depend on the size of the Library's acquisitions budget at a given time. Financial stringency will lead to a perceptible reduction in the quality and coverage of the database. The main sources in regular use in the Social Policy Information Service of the British Library, which between them should cover most aspects of the pure and applied social sciences, are as follows.

Criminology

- **Criminal Justice Abstracts**
  Source: Willow Tree Press
  Available from: SilverPlatter
  Frequency: Quarterly
  Coverage: 1968 to the present
  Print equivalent: *Criminal Justice Abstracts*
  Prepared in co-operation with the Criminal Justice Collection of Rutgers University Library, the database covers journal articles, books, reports and dissertations on vitually every aspect of criminal justice worldwide, including crime trends, crime prevention, juvenile delinquency, juvenile justice, police, courts, punishment and sentencing.

Economics

- **EconLit**
  Source: American Economic Association

Available from: SilverPlatter
Frequency: Quarterly or Monthly
Coverage: 1969 to the present
Print equivalents: *Journal of Economic Literature*; *Index of Economic Articles in Journals and Collective Volumes*; *Abstracts of Working Papers in Economics*.
Provides bibliographic citations, with selected abstracts, to the international literature on economics since 1969. It covers journal articles, books and dissertations as well as articles in collective works such as conference proceedings and collected essay volumes. It includes *Abstracts of Working Papers in Economics* from the Cambridge University Press database, *Index of Economic Articles in Journals and Collective Volumes* and the full text of the *Journal of Economic Literature* book reviews. Topics covered include economic development, forecasting, and history; fiscal theory; monetary theory and financial institutions; business finance; public finance; international, labour, health care, managerial, regional, agricultural and urban economics; country studies and government regulations.

Education and the child

- **ChildData CD-ROM and Online**
  Source: National Children's Bureau
  Available from: Oxmill Publishing
  Frequency: Quarterly
  Print equivalent: *ChildData Abstracts*
  This collection of databases provides a single source of information about all issues affecting children and young people. The *Books, Reports and Journal Articles* file contains details of around 35,000 stock items about children and young people held in the NCB's Library and full text of the most recent 'Highlights' – reviews of research findings on hot topics in the field produced in conjunction with Barnados. *Children in the News* indexes the thousands of stories about children that have appeared in newspapers since 1996. As well as these major databases the resource also includes a directory of organisations active in the field and a searchable calendar of meetings.

- **ERIC**
  Source: US Department of Education Educational Resources Information Center
  Available from: Dialog Corporation and SilverPlatter
  Frequency: Quarterly
  Coverage: 1966 to the present
  Print equivalents: *Current Index to Journals in Education* and *Resources in Education*
  Database consists of two files: *Resources in Education*, which covers research

reports, curriculum and teaching guides, conference papers and books; and *Current Index to Journals in Education* which covers more than 775 international journals in the field of education. It also includes the full text of ERIC Digest Records, which provide a one to two page overview of specific topics for teachers and education administrators.

- **International ERIC**
  Source and available from: Dialog Corporation
  Frequency: Quarterly
  Coverage: 1976 to the present
  Print equivalents: *British Education Index* and *Australian Education Index*
  Subjects covered include counselling, curricula, educational administration, policy, technology and management, multi-cultural education, special education, teacher education, and higher and vocational education. Indexes with brief annotations of academic journals published in the UK and Australia respectively.

Health care management
- **HMIC CD-ROM**
  Source: UK Department of Health; Nuffield Institute, University of Leeds; Kings Fund Library
  Available from: SilverPlatter
  Coverage: 1983 to the present
  Frequency: Quarterly
  Print equivalent: None
  This specialist CD targeting health care management comprises the HELMIS database from the Nuffield Institute which covers health care systems in the UK, Europe and developing countries focusing on health service management, primary care, health care reform, public health and community care; data from the Department of Health which covers health service and hospital administration, medical equipment and supplies, social services, nursing and primary care and public health; and the King's Fund Library database which covers NHS management and organisational development, patient involvement and health care financing and economics.

Political science

*   **International Political Science Abstracts**
    Source: International Political Science Association
    Available from: SilverPlatter
    Frequency: Three times a year
    Coverage: 1989 to the present
    Print equivalent: *International Political Science Abstracts*
    Provides abstracts of articles published in scholarly journals from 1989 to the present. Topics include political thinkers and ideas, political processes (public opinion, political parties and elections), political theory, international relations and national and area studies.

*   **Political Science Abstracts CD-ROM**
    Source: IFI CLAIMS Patent Service
    Available from: SilverPlatter
    Frequency: Quarterly
    Coverage: 1976 to the present
    Print equivalent: *Political Science Abstracts*
    Database contains abstracts of materials from professional journals, major news magazines and books devoted to North American and international politics and political analysis and charts political issues, processes and public policy worldwide.

Social care

*   **AgeInfo CD-ROM**
    Source and available from: Centre for Policy on Ageing
    Frequency: Quarterly
    Print equivalent: None
    The CD-ROM provides a single source of information on all issues affecting older people. It includes CPA's extensive database of references to books, journal articles, statistical sources, research and practice reports and government publications covering the field of older people; a database of information about UK national, European and international organisations active in the field of older people; a searchable calendar of forthcoming and recent short courses, seminars, conferences, training sessions and meetings; and full text of *A Better Home Life*, CPA's code of good practice for residential and nursing home care.

- **CareData CD-ROM and Online**
  Source and available from: National Institute for Social Work
  Frequency: Quarterly
  Print equivalent: *CareData Abstracts*
  Now available online as well as on CD-ROM, CareData gives you access to over 25,000 abstracts of books, reports and journal articles in the field of social care held in the NISW Library, full text of Department of Health circulars and a separate International Social Work Database.

- **Social Work Abstracts Plus CD-ROM**
  Source: National Association of Social Workers
  Available from: SilverPlatter
  Frequency: Quarterly
  Coverage: 1977 to the present
  Print equivalent: *Social Work Abstracts*
  Provides two separate databases on a single disc: *Social Work Abstracts* and the *Register of Clinical Social Workers*. *Social Work Abstracts* indexes more than 450 journals and contains information on all aspects of the profession from a US perspective. The *Register* is a directory of clinical social workers in the United States, and so is of limited use to a UK audience.

Planning and urban issues
- **UrbaDisc CD-ROM**
  Source and available from: Greater London Authority Research Library
  Frequency: Twice a year
  Partial print equivalent: *Urban Abstracts*
  Partial online equivalent: Acompline and Urbaline
  The *UrbaDisc* brings together over 600,000 references on urban and regional planning and policy issues from major databases compiled in Britain, France, Germany, Italy and Spain. The most important databases from the point of view of researchers investigating UK issues are *Acompline* and *Urbaline*. Both emanate from the Greater London Authority Research Library and are based on its collections. *Acompline* offers abstracts of books, research reports and journal articles in the fields of urban and local government affairs, including material on planning, housing, environmental issues, education, transport, leisure and recreation, economic development, community relations and local authority finance and administration. The complementary database *Urbaline* abstracts relevant articles from the quality national daily press. Together these databases contain approximately 160,000 references.

The databases described above constitute only a representative sample of what is available and focus on resources in regular use in the British Library. More online and CD-ROM databases are described in:

- *Gale Directory of Databases*, Detroit: Gale. Two issues per year.

Online searching

Many abstracting, indexing and full text databases in the social sciences can be accessed via commercial hosts such as Dialog and EINS (European Information Network Services). Searches of databases on such hosts would normally be carried out by an information professional on your behalf, as using them effectively requires specialist knowledge and training. They are also very expensive, with searches costing up to £300. If you require an online search, consult the reference staff at your own library to establish which hosts they can access. If your own institution is unable to help, British Library staff will carry out online searches as a fee-based service. For further information contact:

STM Search
British Library
96 Euston Road
London NW1 2DB
Tel: 020 7412 7477
Fax: 020 7412 7954
Email: stm-search@bl.uk

Although costly, commercial hosts offer the benefits of high quality information, advanced information retrieval systems which facilitate precision in searching, and cross file searching of several databases at once.

Chapter 12. Online Journals

The advent of the full text electronic journal offers a quantum leap forward in access to information in all fields. The potential advantages that they offer over print are enormous and include:

- Availability outside of the library via desktop delivery at home and in the office.

- Access twenty-four hours a day, fifty-two weeks a year.

- Immediate guaranteed access, with no delays due to an issue being in use by another reader, at the binders or lost.

- Search and browse access across all the journals to which the library subscribes to locate relevant articles.

- Hotlinks from abstracting and indexing databases to full text of articles in e-journals to which the library subscribes. This facility is already available via ISI's Web of Science and SilverPlatter's Silverlinker service.

- Facilities to cut and paste articles into word processors or email them to yourself for future reference.

Electronic journals are still in their infancy and uptake varies widely from library to library. Almost all electronic journals have a parallel print edition, and the decision on which to take will depend largely on the size of a library's budget and the state of its IT infrastructure.

Libraries will probably provide access to their electronic journals in one or more of these different ways:

- Hotlinks from the Library's catalogue to a specific e-journal title to which it subscribes.

- Hotlinks from an abstracting or indexing database to specific articles in e-journals to which the library subscribes.

- Web-based access to a collection of electronic journals provided by an individual publisher, such as Wiley or Elsevier, a subscription agent such as Swets or Ebsco, or a library consortium such as OCLC. Collections of electronic journals online will normally have the benefit of sophisticated search engines offering Boolean operators, truncation facilities, phrase searching, options to sort results by author, title, date of publication, etc.

Because access to electronic journals is so variable, no review of the strengths and weaknesses of the various providers or modes of provision will be attempted here.

People interested in using fee-based online journals will need to make enquiries as to their availability locally.

As well as subscription-based electronic journals the Internet hosts a number of free titles which can be readily accessed from home. *Sociological Research Online* (**http://www.socresonline.org.uk**) started publication in 1996 and is free to personal users accessing the title through a dial-up account to an Internet Service Provider (ISP), although institutions have to pay. It publishes 'high quality applied sociology, focusing on theoretical, empirical and methodological discussions which engage with current political, cultural and intellectual topics and debates'. As well as offering an archive of scholarly articles, the journal performs a portal function, providing links to the home pages of sociological organisations worldwide, sociology departments in academic institutions worldwide, and other free electronic journals in field.

Increasingly trade journals in field are developing free websites in parallel to their printed editions which offer archives of news items and published articles, current information on jobs and events, links to related websites and directories of organisations in field. The following sample sites are well worth a visit:

- *Community Care* – **http://www.community-care.co.uk** – social care
- *Caring Times* – **http://www.careinfo.org** – long term care
- *Inside Housing* – **http://www.insidehousing.co.uk** – housing
- *Public Finance* – **http://www.publicfinance.co.uk** – public administration
- *Health Service Journal* – **http://www.hsj.co.uk** – health service management
- *Roof* – **http://www.roofmag.org.uk** – housing

Chapter 13. Newspapers

Newspapers are useful as a source of current comment on social issues and problems. The quality press will also announce and summarise major research findings of public interest and government policy initiatives, together with comment and reactions by interested parties. Unfortunately they generally do not provide proper bibliographic citations to their source documents, so you will need to turn detective to follow up the leads they give.

The main archival collection of UK national and regional newspapers is held at the British Library Newspaper Library, Colindale Avenue, London NW9 5HE (Tel: 020 7412 7353; fax: 020 7412 7379; email: newspaper@bl.uk). It also holds selected overseas titles back to the eighteenth century and a range of abstracting and indexing publications.

There are two general indexes to newspapers available in electronic form, one covering the UK and one the US:

- *The British Newspaper Index* (BNI). This electronic index of ten of Britain's quality newspapers covers the *Times*, *The Sunday Times*, *The Financial Times*, *The Independent*, *The Guardian*, *The Observer*, *The Times Literary Supplement*, *The Times Educational Supplement*, *The Times Higher Education Supplement*, *The Daily Mail* and *The Mail on Sunday*. The index is available on CD-ROM from the Gale Group, goes back to 1990 and is updated monthly.

- *Newspaper Abstracts*. Newspaper Abstracts provides cover-to-cover indexing of articles appearing in major US newspapers. The database covering material from 1989 to the present and updated monthly is available in electronic form (CD-ROM or Internet) from SilverPlatter.

Quality newspapers are also available as full text, word searchable databases in electronic form from the early 1990s. Chadwyck-Healey produce CD-ROM versions of the *Financial Times* (from 1990), *The Independent* (from 1990), *The Guardian* and *The Observer* (from 1990), the *Telegraph* (from 1991) and *The Times* and *Sunday Times* (from 1990). *FT Profile*, one of Europe's most extensive news and current affairs online hosts, provides access to full text of UK, US and European newspapers, magazines and news wires, with a business and economic bias. Those without other access to *Profile* may request a charged online search through:

Business Information Research Service
British Library
96 Euston Road
London NW1 2DB

Tel: 020 7412 7457
Fax: 020 7412 7453
Email: business-information@bl.uk

or

Dialtech
British Library
96 Euston Road
London NW1 2DB
Tel: 020 7412 7951
Fax: 020 7412 7954
Email: dialtech@bl.uk

Finally, all the British quality daily newspapers have free websites where more or less complete internet editions are available. These include:

- *Guardian*
  http://www.newsunlimited.co.uk/guardian
  Available over the NewsUnlimited network, with a searchable archive back to 1 September 1998.

- *Independent*
  http://www.independent.co.uk
  News of the day with an archive from October 1999.

- *Financial Times*
  http://www.ft.com
  The newly relaunched website provides information via six channels: news and analysis, markets and portfolio, careers (workplace trends), community (discussion forum), time-off (leisure guides), and search and archive (access to a search engine and web directory of business sources).

- *Times*
  http://www.the-times.co.uk
  Offers access to back issues from 1 January 1996, useful compilations of articles on hot topics such as the New Deal, and search facilities.

- *Electronic Telegraph*
  http://www.telegraph.co.uk
  Substantial proportion of the printed *Daily Telegraph* with a searchable archive back to 1994.

Chapter 14. Developing a Search Strategy

To get the best value from searching any of the electronic sources described above, it is well worthwhile spending some time in preparing your search strategy in advance.

The first step in preparing a search is to choose the most appropriate sources. Consult your reference librarian for advice on what databases and other resources are available locally. You should then consult any documentation available which describes the resources, including user manuals for CD-ROMs, Internet guides to free databases, and database descriptions issued by commercial online hosts. These will help you to determine the most appropriate database for your search.

Having chosen the databases you intend to use, prepare your search on paper. Begin by breaking down your query into discrete concepts. For example, if you are looking for information on preschool education for deprived children in London, you have three concepts in play:

1   deprived children

2   preschool education

3   London

Next consider how the database you are going to use is indexed. Whether or not it uses controlled subject indexing terms taken from a thesaurus will heavily influence the development of your search strategy. A thesaurus, in librarianship terms, offers a set of verbal descriptors that ensures that subjects in a database or catalogue are consistently described. The thesaurus will designate a preferred term to be used to describe a given concept and will cross-refer from synonyms. Thus deprived children can also be described as poor children and disadvantaged children. A thesaurus would designate one of these as the preferred descriptor to be consistently used by indexers, making *See* references from the others. The thesaurus will also indicate broader, narrower and related terms that can be used to expand your search. If your database uses controlled vocabulary, then consult the thesaurus to choose your search terms.

If your database is not indexed using a controlled vocabulary, then you yourself will need to think of synonyms and alternative ways of describing your subject to ensure a comprehensive search. You will need to think of:

*   Synonyms

*   Broader/narrower terms

*   Abbreviations, eg UK for United Kingdom

- Alternative spellings, English and American forms

- Plurals

- Different word forms, eg police, policing

- Variants due to hyphenation, eg preschool, pre-school

Applying this to our example of 'Preschool education of deprived children in London', three sets of terms would be developed:

Deprived children	Preschool education	London
Disadvantaged children	Pre-school education	Islington
Poor children	Nursery education	Hackney, etc
	Under fives education	

The next step is to combine the words and phrases that define your search using Boolean operators:

- AND retrieves records where concept A AND concept B both occur eg residential AND care will search for records where the words residential and care both occur

- OR retrieves records where either concept A OR concept B OR both occur, eg abuse OR neglect will search for records where either the word abuse or the word neglect occur

- NOT retrieves records where the concept A occurs independently of concept B, eg illness NOT mental will retrieve records where the word illness occurs but will exclude those also containing the word mental.

So combining our sets of terms using Boolean AND and OR would produce:

String 1	*String 2*	*String 3*
Deprived children	Preschool education	London
OR	OR	OR
Disadvantaged children	Pre-school education	Islington
OR	OR	OR
Poor children	Nursery education	Hackney
	OR	
	Under fives education	

Next run each of these strings in turn as a separate search against your database and then combine the results of the three searches using the Boolean operator AND:

Set 1 AND Set 2 AND Set 3

In some databases the same result can be got using brackets to combine different Boolean operators in the same string:

> (Deprived children OR Disadvantaged children OR Poor children) AND (Preschool education OR Nursery education OR Under fives education) AND (London OR Islington OR Hackney)

When you first carry out your search using your carefully formulated search string, one of two results is likely. Either you will retrieve an overwhelming number of hits, many of which will be irrelevant or you will retrieve too few references. Remedial action can be taken in both cases.

To reduce the number of hits you can:

- Add more terms using the AND operator to make the search more precise, eg bullying AND workplace would retrieve fewer hits than just 'bullying' as references to bullying in schools would be excluded.

- Limit your search to documents in a certain language, or published within a given date range, eg documents in English only published between 1990 and 2000.

- Limit your search to a specific part of the record such as the title or the controlled subject descriptors rather than searching the whole record.

- Search for phrases rather than linking terms using the Boolean AND. For example, searching for the phrase 'aviation management' would exlude records where the word 'aviation' and the word 'management' occur separately in different parts of the record as in a report on *Air Traffic Management in the UK* by the Civil Aviation Authority.

- Search using more specific or narrower terms, eg nuclear family instead of family structure.

To increase the number of hits you can:

- Try a different database – your choice of file may be inappropriate

- Try alternative words and phrases such as synonyms, abbreviations, or variant spellings. Thus you could broaden a search for older people in Britain by adding such terms as elderly people, senior citizens, pensioners, aged people to your search statement using the Boolean OR operator. To expand on Britain, you could add United Kingdom, UK, England, Scotland, Wales, GB, etc., again linking them using Boolean OR.

- Use truncation to retrieve words with variant endings at one fell swoop. Assuming that the truncation symbol is an asterisk (*) in the database you are searching currently, child* would retrieve child, children, childish.

- Use wildcard searching to retrieve words with variant spellings. Assuming the wildcard symbol is a question mark (?), Organi?ation would retrieve organisation and organization.

- Try searching using broader terms. If you are researching insomnia and find insufficient material using it as your search term, then try a search using a broader term such as sleep disorders. A document on sleep disorders in general may contain relevant material on insomnia in particular.

- Browse online indexes, if available, to identify controlled vocabulary. You may be getting no hits because you are searching using a non-preferred term. It is no use searching on 'Job stress' as a subject descriptor if your database is using the term 'Occupational stress' to index the concept. Online indexes will in many cases direct you to the preferred term via cross-references.

In all cases, familiarise yourself with the search conventions, tools and functionality available on your database by a thorough study of the User Guide before you start. CD-ROM titles and online databases designed for end-user searching are accessed through as many different search interfaces as there are publishers. Knowing their quirks before you start will save time and temper.

Appendix. Publishers' Contact Details

The following list gives the addresses, phone numbers and websites (where known) of the publishing organisations mentioned in the body of the text.

American Library Association
50 E Huron
Chicago, Ill. 60611
Tel: (800) 545 2433
Website: **http://www.ala.org**

Aslib
Staple Hall
Stone House Court
London EC3A 7PB
Tel: 020 7903 0000
Website: **http://www.aslib.co.uk**

Association of Commonwealth Universities
John Foster House
36 Gordon Square
London WC1H 0PF
Tel: 020 7387 8572
Website: **http://www.acu.ac.uk**

Beechwood House Publishing
Grover House
Grover Walk
Corringham
Essex SS17 7LS
Tel: 01375 644344
Website: **http://www.binleys.com**

Bell & Howell Information and Learning
300 North Zeeb Road
PO Box 1346
Ann Arbor
Michigan 48106 1346
Tel: (734) 761 4700
Website: **http://www.umi.com**

Bernan Press
4611-F Assembly Drive
Lanham, Md 20706 4391
Tel: (301) 459 2255
Website: **http://www.bernan.com**

R R Bowker
121 Chanlon Road
New Providence
New Jersey 07974
Tel: (888) 269 5372
Website: **http:// www.bowker.com**

Bowker Saur
Windsor Court
East Grinstead House
East Grinstead
West Sussex RH19 1XA
Tel: 01342 336145
Website: **http://www.bowker-saur.co.uk**

British Institute of Learning Disabilities
Information and Resources
Wolverhampton Road
Kidderminster
Worcs DY10 3PP
Tel: 01562 850251
Website: **http://www.bild.org.uk**

British Library
BSDS Publications
Boston Spa
Wetherby
West Yorks LS23 7BQ
Tel: 01937 546585
Website: **http://www.bl.uk**

British Library
Document Supply Centre
Customer Services
Boston Spa
Wetherby
West Yorks LS23 7BQ
Tel: 01937 546060
Website: **http://www.bl.uk**

British Library
Publishing Office
96 Euston Road
London NW1 2DB
Tel: 020 7412 7472
Website: **http://www.bl.uk**

British Official Publications Current
Awareness Service
Ford Collection of British Official Publications
Hartley Library
University of Southampton
Highfield
Southampton SO17 1BJ
Tel: 023 8059 2370
Website: **http://www.bopcas.com**

CBD Research
Chancery House
15 Wickham Road
Beckenham
Kent BR3 5JS
Tel: 020 8650 7745
Website: **http://www.glen.co.uk/cbd**

Centre for Policy on Ageing
25-31 Ironmonger Row
London EC1V 3QP
Tel: 020 7253 1787
Website: **http://www.cpa.org.uk**

Chadwyck-Healey Ltd
The Quorum
Barnwell Road
Cambridge
CB5 8SW
Tel: 01223 215512
Website: **http://www.chadwyck.co.uk**

Community of Science Inc
18 Allnutt Way
London SW4 9RF
Tel: 020 7498 1820
Website: **http://www.cos.com**

Congressional Information Service
4520 East-West Highway
Bethesda MD 20814-3389
Tel: (301) 654 1550
Website: **http://www.cispubs.com**

Context Ltd
20 Kentish Town Road
London NW1 9NR
Tel: 020 7267 8989
Website: **http://www.context.co.uk**

Department of Health
Health Service Abstracts
Room 5CO7
Quarry House
Quarry Hill
Leeds LS2 7UE
Tel: 0113 254 5072/4
Website: **http://www.doh.gov.uk**

Dialog Corporation
Dialog On Disc Division
2 Des Roches Square
Witney
Oxford OX8 6BE
Tel: 01993 899300
Website: **http://www.dialog.com**

Economic and Social Research Council
Polaris House
North Star Avenue
Swindon 5NZ 1UJ
Tel: 01793 413000
Website: **http://www.esrc.ac.uk**

Euromonitor
60-61 Britton Street
London EC1M 5UX
Tel : 020 7251 8024
Website: **http://www.euromonitor.com**

Europa Publications
Newspaper House
Great New Street
London EC4P 4EE
Tel: 020 7822 4300
Website: **http://www.europapublications.com**

Financial Times Business Directories
Maple House
149 Tottenham Court Road
London W1P 9LL
Tel: 020 7896 2359
Website: **http://www.directories.ft.com**

Fitzroy Dearborn
919 North Michigan Avenue
Suite 760
Chicago
Illinois 60611
Tel: (312) 587 0131
Website: **http://www.fitzroydearborn.com**

Gale Group
27500 Drake Road
Farmington Hills
Michigan 48331
Tel: (248) 699 4253
Website: **http://www.gale.com**

Greater London Authority Research Library
81 Black Prince Road
London SE1 7SZ
Tel: 020 7983 4666
Website: **http://www.london-research.gov.uk**

R Hazell & Co
PO Box 39
Henley-on-Thames
Oxon RG9 5UA

Hollis Directories
Harlequin House
7 High Street
Teddington
Middlesex TW11 8EL
Tel: 020 8977 7711
Website: **http://www.hollis-pr.co.uk**

Institute for Scientific Information
ISI Europe
Brunel Science Park
Uxbridge UB8 3PQ
Tel: 01895 270016
Website: **http://www.isinet.com**

Institute for Volunteering Research
c/o National Centre for Volunteering
Regents Wharf
8 All Saints Street
London N1 9RL
Tel: 020 7520 8900
Website: **http://www.volunteering.org.uk**

Landmarks Sa
Avenue de Tervuren 402
1150 Brussels
Belgium
Tel: (+32) 2 779 95 49
Website: **http://www.landmarks.be**

Library Association
7 Ridgmount Street
London WC1E 7AE
Tel: 020 7255 0594
Website: **http://www.la-hq.org.uk**

Macmillan Press
Brunel Road
Houndmills
Basingstoke
Hants RG21 6XS
Tel: 01256 329242
Website: **http://www.macmillan.com**

Marshall Cavendish
99 White Plain's Road
PO Box 2001
Tarrytown
New York 10591
Tel: (914) 332 8888
Website: **http://www.marshallcavendish.com**

National Association of Social Workers
750 First Street NE Suite 700
Washington DC 20002-4241
Tel: (202) 408 8600
Website: **http://www.naswdc.org**

National Children's Bureau
8 Wakley Street
London EC1V 7QE
Tel: 020 7843 6008
Website: **http://www.ncb.org.uk**

National Council for Voluntary Organisations
Regents Wharf
8 All Saints Street
London N1 9RL
Tel: 020 7713 6161
Website: **http://www.ncvo-vol.org.uk**

National Institute for Social Work
5 Tavistock Place
London WC1H 9SN
Tel: 020 7387 9681
Website: **http://www.nisw.org.uk**

National Institute of Adult Continuing Education
21 De Montfort Street
Leicester LE1 7GE
Tel: 0116 2044200
Website: **http://www.niace.org.uk**

Newman Books
32 Vauxhall Bridge Road
London SW1V 2SS
Tel: 020 7973 6402
Website: **http://www.newmanbooks.co.uk**

Oxford University Press
Great Clarendon Street
Oxford OX2 6DP
Tel: 01865 556767
Website: **http://www.oup.co.uk**

Oxmill Publishing
Croudace House
97 Godstone Road
Caterham
Surrey CR3 6RE
Tel: 01883 343000
Website: **http://www.oxmill.com**

Pinter
Wellington House
125 The Strand
London WC2R 0BB

Planning Exchange
Tontine House
8 Gordon Street
Glasgow G1 3PL
Tel: 0141 248 8541
Website: **http://www.planex.co.uk**

Primary Source Media
50 Milford Road
Reading RG1 8LJ
Tel: 0118 9577211
Website: **http://www.psmedia.com**

Reed Business Information
Community Care
Quadrant House
The Quadrant
Sutton
Surrey SM2 5AS
Tel: 020 8652 4861/4699/4859
Website: **http://www.community-care.co.uk**

Routledge
11 New Fetter Lane
London EC4P 4EE
Tel: 020 7583 9855
Website: **http://www.routledge.com**

Royal National Institute for the Blind
Research Library
224 Great Portland Street
London W1N 6AA
Tel: 020 7391 2052
Website: **http://www.rnib.org.uk**

K G Saur Verlag
Ortlerstrasse 8
D-81373 Munchen
Germany
Tel: (+49) 89 76902 0
Website: **http://www.saur.de**

M E Sharpe Inc
80 Business Park Drive
Armonk NY 10504
Tel: (800) 541 6563
Website: **http://www.mesharpe.com**

Shaw and Sons Ltd
21 Bourne Park
Bourne Road
Crayford
Kent DA1 4BZ
Tel: 01322 621100
Website: **http://www.shaws.co.uk**

Silver Platter Information
Merlin House
20 Belmont Terrace
Chiswick
London W4 5UG
Tel: 020 8585 6400
Website: **http://www.silverplatter.com**

The Stationery Office
PO Box 29
Norwich NR3 1GN
Tel: 0870 600 5522
Website: **http://www.ukstate.com**

University Microfilms International
See Bell & Howell Information and Learning
Waterlow Professional Publishing
Paulton House
8 Shepherdess Walk
London N1 7LB
Tell: 020 7490 0049
Website: **http://www.waterlow.com**

Westview Press
12 Hid's Copse Road
Cumnor Hill
Oxford OX2 9JJ
Tel: 01865 865466
Website: **http://www.westviewpress.com**

John Wiley
Baffins Lane
Chichester
West Sussex PO19 1UD
Tel: 01243 779777
Website: **http://www.wiley.com**

H W Wilson
950 University Avenue
Bronx
New York 10452
Tel: (718) 588 8400
Website: **http://www.hwwilson.com**

World Bank
1818 H Street NW
Washington DC 20433
Tel: (202) 477 1234
Website: **http://www.worldbank.org**